A Sea of Animals

by Janine Scott

Content and Reading Adviser: Joan Stewart
Educational Consultant/Literacy Specialist
New York Public Schools

 COMPASS POINT BOOKS

Minneapolis, Minnesota

Compass Point Books
3109 West 50th Street, #115
Minneapolis, MN 55410

Visit Compass Point Books on the Internet at *www.compasspointbooks.com*
or e-mail your request to *custserv@compasspointbooks.com*

Photographs ©:
DigitalVision, cover; Corel, 4, 5 (frogfish); PhotoDisc, 5 (jellyfish); Visuals Unlimited/David Wrobel, 6;
Visuals Unlimited/William J. Weber, 7; PhotoDisc, 9; Corel, 10, 11; PhotoDisc, 12; Two Coyote
Studios/Mary Walker Foley, 13; PhotoDisc, 14; DigitalVision, 15, 16; Two Coyote Studios/Mary Walker
Foley, 17; PhotoDisc, 18; Visuals Unlimited/Glenn M. Oliver, 19; PhotoDisc, 20 (sea otter); Two Coyote
Studios/Mary Walker Foley, 20 (starfish); Corel, 21.

Project Manager: Rebecca Weber McEwen
Editor: Jennifer Waters
Photo Researcher: Jennifer Waters
Photo Selectors: Rebecca Weber McEwen and Jennifer Waters
Designer: Mary Walker Foley

Library of Congress Cataloging-in-Publication Data

Scott, Janine.
  A sea of animals / by Janine Scott.
    p. cm. -- (Spyglass books)
Includes bibliographical references (p.   ),
  ISBN 0 7565 0240-9 (hardcover)
  1. Marine animals--Juvenile literature. [1. Marine animals.] I.
Title. II. Series.
  QL122 .S36 2002
  591.77--dc21

                          2001007336

Contents

A Sea of Animals

Many animals live in
the ocean.
Some live in warm waters.
Others live in deep,
cold waters.

Tropical fish

Frogfish

Jellyfish

5

Life on the Edge

Some animals live in tide pools at the edge of the ocean. They hide under rocks or in seaweed while the tide is out.

Tide pool

Crab

Light to Dark Waters

The top layer of the ocean is the warmest. The middle layer does not get much sunlight. It is cooler. The bottom layer is the coldest. There is very little sunlight there.

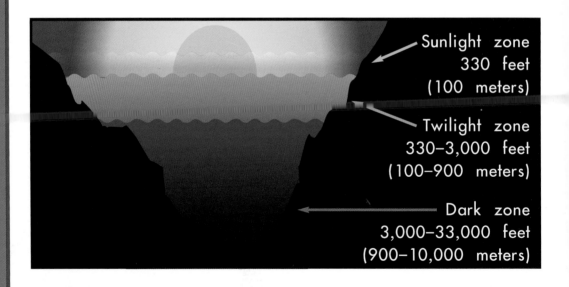

Sunlight zone
330 feet
(100 meters)

Twilight zone
330–3,000 feet
(100–900 meters)

Dark zone
3,000–33,000 feet
(900–10,000 meters)

Sunlight shining
through the water

Dining in the Deep

Some ocean animals wait for dinner to float past. Some animals hunt for their food. Other animals, such as sea cows, graze on sea grasses that grow on the sandy ocean floor.

Shrimp are food for many animals.

Sea cow

11

Interesting Creatures

The ocean has many kinds of animals. There are **mammals**, such as seals, whales, and walruses.
There are **reptiles**, such as sea snakes and sea turtles.

A sea turtle is a reptile.

A seal is a mammal.

How Do They Live?

Animals that live in the **Arctic** and **Antarctic** Oceans have a layer of **blubber** or thick, oily feathers to protect them from these icy waters.

Dolphins have a layer of blubber.

Penguins have thick, oily feathers.

Seabirds fly over the ocean, then dive under the water to catch their food.

Seabirds have webbed feet for swimming. Oily feathers keep them warm.

Seagulls

This seagull has webbed feet.

Journeys in the Sea

Some ocean animals, such as anemones, do not travel anywhere during their lives. Other animals, such as humpback whales, travel great distances in the ocean to find food and raise their young.

Anemone

Humpback whale

Fun Facts

If one of a starfish's arms breaks off, it can grow another one.

Sea otters eat shellfish, such as clams. They smash the shells open by hitting them against a rock.

If a shark
stops swimming, it will sink.

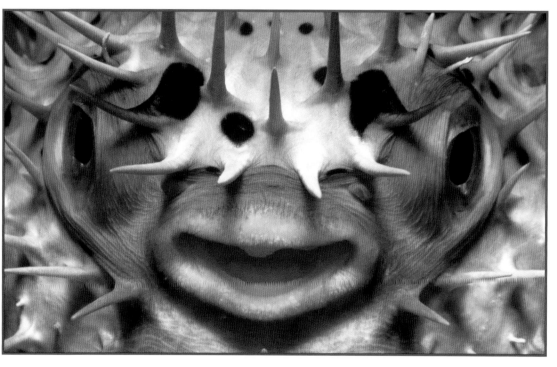

To scare away hunters, such as sharks,
the porcupine fish sucks in water to
appear twice its normal size and to
make its spines stick out!

Glossary

Antarctic—describes the area at and around the South Pole

Arctic—describes the area at and around the North Pole

blubber—a layer of fat under the skin of certain sea animals

mammal—a warm-blooded animal that grows hair. Female mammals produce milk for their young.

reptile—an animal that breathes air and is usually covered with scales or plates

Learn More

Books

Martin-James, Kathleen. *Floating Jellyfish.* Minneapolis, Minn.: Lerner Publications, 2001.

Schaefer, Lola M. *Sea Stars.* Mankato, Minn.: Pebble Books, 1999.

Theodorou, Rod. *Fish.* Des Plaines, Ill.: Heinemann Library, 2000.

On the Web

For more information on sea animals, use FactHound.

1. Go to *www.facthound.com*
2. Type in a search word related to this book or this book ID: 0756502403
3. Click on the *Fetch It* button.

FactHound will fetch the best Web sites for you!

Index

GR: G
Word Count: 213

From Janine Scott

I live in New Zealand, and have two daughters. They love to read fact books that are full of fun facts and features. I hope you do, too!